Bumblebees

naturally scottish

SCOTTISH
NATURAL
HERITAGE

IN MEMORY

Dave Phillips of SNH sadly died in
December 2003. Dave initiated the
project, advised on the text and
illustrations, and this publication is a
tribute to his bright enthusiasm for all
invertebrates.

Acknowledgements: David Phillips for advice and comments

Author: Murdo Macdonald

Series Editor: Lynne Farrell (SNH)

Design and production: SNH Design and Publications

Photographs:

Ted Benton front cover, frontispiece, 2 top, 2 centre top, 2 centre bottom, 2 bottom, 4, 6, 8, 13, 14, 20, 21, 22, 31 left;
Bob Gibbons/Oxford Scientific Films 25; **Lorne Gill/SNH** back cover bottom right, 17, 18, 23, 29 top left, 29 top right, 29 bottom left,
29 bottom right, 30, 31 right, 32; **Natural History Photographic Agency** 9; **Steve Littlewood/Oxford Scientific Films** 7;
Gordon Maclean/Oxford Scientific Films viii; **Oxford Bee Company** 28; **OSF/Oxford Scientific Films** back cover top left,
Peter O'Toole/Oxford Scientific Films 12

Illustrations:

Kelly Stuart/SNH 10 & 15

Scottish Natural Heritage
Design and Publications
Battleby
Redgorton
Perth PH1 3EW
Tel: 01738 444177
Fax: 01738 827411
E-mail: pubs@snh.gov.uk
Web site: http://www.snh.org.uk

Cover photograph:
Male Buff-tailed Bumblebee (*Bombus terrestris*) on creeping thistle

Frontispiece:
Garden Bumblebee (*Bombus hortorum*) dusted with pollen on sage

Back cover photograph:
White-tailed Bumblebee (*Bombus lucorum*) on French marigold

Bumblebees

naturally scottish

by

Murdo Macdonald

Foreword

A naturalist's experience is greatly enhanced by appreciating the biodiversity of insects, as well as other animals and plants. Among insects, bumblebees are one of the most attractive and rewarding of groups. They are large, colourful and often easy to identify without capture. As well as contributing aesthetically to our quality of life, they are valuable as pollinators, particularly on some crops and wild flowers that honeybees do not pollinate effectively. This publication is timely, because informed local habitat management may yet redress the decline of several bumblebee species in Britain.

Bumblebees are numerous in a range of habitats from urban gardens to moors and woodland rides. The commoner species are abundant enough to provide continuous interest, and the rarer species rare enough to provide sporadic excitement. As well as giving a guide to literature for identification, this publication will help observers to interpret the bumblebees' activities. It will reveal the significance of a humming crowd of queen bumblebees collecting nectar on sallow catkins in spring, or a solitary male patrolling a regular route in summer, pausing at a particular leaf and perhaps anointing it with scent, or a forager pushing her tongue into a deep flower through a hole bitten in the base of the petals.

Murdo Macdonald's enjoyable text, complemented by the excellent photographs, will surely tempt many people to study and enjoy this fascinating group of insects. It will enrich their explorations of natural history by unveiling the fascinating complexity of the foraging habitats and social life of bumblebees. It may stimulate readers to cherish landscape elements important to bumblebees, such as tussocky grassland used for nesting and established flowery places where they find food.

Sarah A Corbet

Sarah A Corbet
Bumblebee specialist and former zoology lecturer at the University of Cambridge

Garden Bumblebee (*Bombus hortorum*) with a full pollen load takes flight

Contents

Male White-tailed Bumblebee (*Bombus lucorum*) feeding on ragwort

Introduction

What is special about Bumblebees?

To the general public, bumblebees, because of their distinctive appearance and close association with humans, are probably the best-loved insects after butterflies. They feature as instantly recognisable caricatures in commercial logos and children's books, usually with a human-like smiling face that you will not find in reality. As is evident when they are drawn disappearing into wooden hives, they are often confused with their relative the honeybee.

To the naturalist, bumblebees are of crucial importance as pollinators of wild flowers, and because they depend on the presence of an abundant and diverse flora, they are useful indicators of the health of the environment. If you find lots of bumblebees, there is likely to be an abundance of other wildlife too. Bumblebees are important economically as pollinators of commercial fruit and vegetables. Indeed, there is an international trade in bumblebee colonies for use in glass-houses.

Bumblebees act as hosts for many parasites, and several kinds of insects - moths, beetles, hoverflies - live together with the bumblebees in their nests, surviving on the debris and causing no great harm. (Parasites are organisms which feed off other living plants or animals, the parasite gaining some benefit while the other organism, the host, is harmed).

I trust my first publication may cause someone at least to search into this overlooked & despised nook of the Animal Kingdom. It is, I believe, because the Humble Bee's first cousin the Honey Bee is so spoilt by human help & praise that she herself fades into insignificance. However, in the following pages I mean to point out that Humble Bees are extremely interesting if not profitable to Man.

From the Preface of a hand-written booklet produced in 1892 and sold for sixpence by Frederick Sladen, author of the classic The Humble-bee, when he was 16 years old.

Bumblebee names

Scottish name:

Bummer, bumbee, bummiebee, bummle, bumbard, from 'bum' meaning to hum. Droner is another reference to the sound.

Donner-bee is less complimentary, meaning 'stupid'.

Baker-bee, dusty miller are used for the Common Carder Bee, its brown colour reminiscent of the brown coats worn by bakers in the past.

Foggie-toddler is a Deeside name. 'Fog' is Scots for moss or grass, and 'toddling' is meandering with a gentle sound. Also foggie-bee, foggie-bummer and todler-tyke.

Gaelic name:

Seillean-mòr is pronounced 'shellen' with the stress on the first syllable. Mòr is Gaelic for 'large'.

English names:

Bumblebee, humblebee both derive from the sound made by their wings.

Latin names:

Bombus means 'booming' and *Psithyrus* means 'murmuring' - referring to the sound made in flight.

Northern White-tailed Bumblebee *Bombus magnus*

Early Bumblebee *Bombus pratorum*

Red-tailed Bumblebee *Bombus lapidarius*

Common Carder Bee *Bombus pascuorum*

English name		Latin name	
Broken-belted Bumblebee	Refers to the broken yellow abdominal band	Bombus soroeensis	Named after Soröe in Denmark where it was discovered
White-tailed Bumblebee	But not the only one with a white tail	Bombus lucorum	From Latin 'lucus' - a copse
Northern White-tailed Bumblebee	Commonest in the north and west	Bombus magnus	Latin for 'large', but it is not especially so
Buff-tailed Bumblebee	But workers have white tails	Bombus terrestris	Nests in holes in the earth (Latin 'terra')
Heath Bumblebee	This bee is not confined to heaths...	Bombus jonellus	Named in honour of an entomologist D. Jones
Bilberry Bumblebee	... nor this one to Bilberry	Bombus monticola	Latin for 'living in the mountains'
Early Bumblebee	The first species to complete its cycle	Bombus pratorum	From Latin 'pratus' - a meadow
Red-tailed Bumblebee	Several bumblebees have a red tail	Bombus lapidarius	'Lapis' means stone - it sometimes nests in stone walls
Garden Bumblebee	Not confined to gardens, nor the commonest there	Bombus hortorum	From Latin 'hortus' - a garden
Moss Carder Bee	'Carder' refers to their nest building - like carding wool	Bombus muscorum	From Latin 'musca' - moss
Common Carder Bee	This is a very common bee	Bombus pascuorum	From Latin 'pascuum' - a pasture
Red-shanked Carder Bee	It has red pollen baskets	Bombus ruderarius	From Latin 'rudus' - rubble
Great Yellow Bumblebee	Less yellow than some	Bombus distinguendus	Distinctive and distinguished
Gypsy Cuckoo Bumblebee	An extension from 'bohemian'	Bombus (Psithyrus) bohemicus	Named after the region in E Europe
Barbut's Cuckoo Bumblebee		Bombus (Psithyrus) barbutellus	Named after the discoverer
Field Cuckoo Bumblebee	A translation of the Latin	Bombus (Psithyrus) campestris	From Latin 'campus' - a field
Forest Cuckoo Bumblebee	Most often found in or near forests	Bombus (Psithyrus) sylvestris	From Latin 'sylvus' - a forest or wood

Most books on bumblebees use Latin names. This table matches the English names used in this book to the Latin names used elsewhere.

How they feed

Bumblebees as pollinators

Millions of years ago, as flowering plants evolved, primitive plants and early insects arrived at an evolutionary 'agreement' that gives some of the best examples of mutualism - two different species working together for their mutual benefit. The plants were food for insects. As insects picked up pollen grains (which contain the male sex cells) at random and moved on, transferring them to the female reproductive structures of other plants, some strains reproduced better than others. Features which assisted transfer of pollen by insects were favoured.

Those individual flowers which had the largest glands or nectaries, and which excreted most nectar, would be oftenest visited by insects, and would be oftenest crossed; and so in long run would gain the upper hand. Those flowers, also, which had their stamens and pistils placed, in relation to the size and habits of the particular insects which visited them, so as to favour in any degree the transportal of their pollen from flower to flower, would likewise be favoured or selected.
Charles Darwin, 1859, The Origin of Species

Eventually, plants evolved modified leaves to take on the functions of attracting insects by their colours and patterns. Chemicals which had perhaps served other uses in the plants were employed as scent lures. Special glands (nectaries) took on the sole function of secreting sugary sap as a food supply for the visitors; and protein-rich pollen grains were produced in superabundance, so that the insects were provided with a balanced diet without endangering the plant's reproductive interests.

In return, the insects took on the specialist rôle of pollen transfer, ensuring successful reproduction of the plants, and a plentiful supply of fruits and seeds for many birds and mammals - including ourselves. In the process, some insects, including the bumblebees, became totally dependent on flowers for food. On the other hand, many plants, for example red clover, are largely dependent on bumblebees for pollination and the monk's-hoods are completely dependent on long-tongued bumblebees.

Moss Carder Bee (*Bombus muscorum*) with full pollen baskets on red clover

I have, also, reason to believe that humble-bees are indispensable to the fertilisation of the heartsease, for other bees do not visit this flower. I have found that the visits of bees, if not indispensable, are at least highly beneficial to the fertilisation of our clovers; but humble-bees alone visit the common red clover, as other bees cannot reach the nectar. Hence I have very little doubt, that if the whole genus of humble-bees became extinct or very rare in England, the heartsease and red clover would become very rare, or wholly disappear.

Charles Darwin, 1859, The Origin of Species

The first successful attempts to introduce the bumblebees were made by the Canterbury Acclimatization Society in 1885 and 1886, when 93, out of a total of 442 queens shipped from England, reached New Zealand alive. The cost of importing these live queens worked out at 9/5d. each, but they soon paid for themselves since the increase in the bumblebee population during the next few years was phenomenally rapid ... and the red clover seed-crop increased considerably.

Free & Butler, 1959, Bumblebees

Bumblebees are supreme among the insect pollinators in Scotland. They are active in weather that keeps honeybees at home - a significant factor in the Scottish climate - helped by their ability to absorb heat from even weak sunlight and retain it in their hair-insulated bodies. The hairs are finely branched, allowing pollen grains to stick very easily. Their relatively long tongues can reach deep stores of nectar which they suck into a special 'honey-stomach' which may hold well over 50 percent of their body weight.

Red-shanked Carder Bee (*Bombus ruderarius*) on sneezewort

6

Foraging

When queens emerge in spring, they have never seen the flowers on offer, having experienced only those of late summer. Each individual queen must learn which flowers allow it to feed efficiently. Bumblebee workers are able to share information on the type of forage plants. However, unlike honeybees, they cannot share information on their location. Their 'aim' is to get close to optimal foraging - getting as much food of the right sort as necessary in the least time.

Sometimes choice of flower is dictated by the length of the tongue relative to the depth of the flower. Short-tongued bees cannot reach nectar in the long tube of honeysuckle, but the long-tongued Garden Bumblebee drinks it easily. The Buff-tailed and White-tailed Bumblebees, however, often 'steal' from the spurs of columbine, biting through the spur and drinking nectar that they could not reach otherwise.

Nectar is sucked up by the 'tongue' - a complex structure with an absorbent tip and a channel like a drinking-straw. The bees comb pollen off their bodies at intervals, pack it into semi-solid masses in the pollen-baskets on their hind legs, and take it to the nest to be stored in wax cells for the larvae to eat. Usually, pollen will be collected at the same flowers as provide nectar, but some flowers (for example roses, gorse, broom) have no nectar and are visited only for pollen.

Male bumblebees forage only for themselves, and require energy-rich nectar rather than pollen, so appear distinctly more sluggish than workers. Males often feed at different flowers from their females, partly because they are active at different seasons, and partly because of their different dietary requirements.

Some species will feed on 'honeydew' - the sugary excreta of aphids and other plant-sucking bugs - when they find large colonies of these insects.

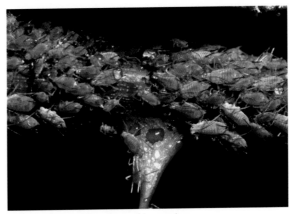

Aphid colony with a drop of honeydew

Bumblebees store a small volume of rather watery honey (regurgitated nectar) in the nest in a special wax cell called the 'honeypot'. Since bumblebee colonies do not last the winter, their stores serve only the immediate needs of the colony, perhaps to tide them over a few days of poor weather when foraging is difficult. There is enough, however, to have attracted the hay reapers in days when farming was less mechanised than now. Many old farmers and crofters tell how they would drink the honey from nests found while they worked in the hay meadows.

Even in the 'sixties my good and faithful grieve John Grant, when at the head of his squad (long before mowing machines were ever thought of), used to be quite annoyed at the continual hindrance to the scythe work through men stopping to raid bees' nests in the grass, and losing time in eating the honey and the ceir (bee-bread), and pretending they could not go back to their work owing to the attacks of the infuriated bees. My old sheep manager ... owned a collie dog in the 'sixties which learned to point at bees' nests. On one occasion when he was taking quite a short turn on one of his beats on my property his dog found thirty bees' nests for him, some of which contained quite a saucerful of honey and bee-bread.

Osgood Mackenzie (the creator of Inverewe Gardens in Wester Ross), 1921, A Hundred Years in the Highlands. It is not clear what species of bee was involved, but it is likely from the location of the nests that they were Carder Bees. The 'sixties referred to in the quote are the 1860s.

Male Broken-belted Bumblebee (*Bombus soroeensis*) on knapweed

Inside a nest of White-tailed Bumblebees (*Bombus lucorum*) with honeypots (left) and brood cells tended by workers

How they breed

Bumblebee biology

Bumblebee colonies last only for one season, unlike honeybees which have perennial hives. As the ground warms up in spring, queen bumblebees begin to stir in their winter retreats. The first bees to appear in spring - the only ones alive at that time of year - are queens (breeding females), which have hibernated after mating the previous year. They need to replenish the stores of fat that have sustained them through the winter, and spend much time drinking nectar - an energy-rich sugary solution - and eating pollen, which provides protein for the developing eggs, at suitable flowers.

Later, they collect pollen and carry it in the pollen baskets on their hind legs to their chosen nest-site in a hole in the ground or at the base of a rank grass tussock. They store the pollen in wax cells in the nest to provide food for their larvae, and begin to lay eggs and incubate them rather as birds do. The first eggs are fertilised normally, and they develop into females which will not breed. These are the workers. As the workers take over the foraging, bringing supplies of nectar and pollen to the nest, the queen spends most of her time in the nest laying eggs. The workers maintain the nest and tend the larvae. Some workers, indeed, never leave the nest at all.

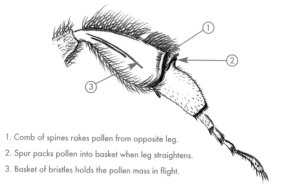

1. Comb of spines rakes pollen from opposite leg.
2. Spur packs pollen into basket when leg straightens.
3. Basket of bristles holds the pollen mass in flight.

The hind leg of a female bumblebee is designed to carry pollen

Four or five weeks of labour have told heavily on the queen; the tips of her wings have become torn and tattered, and when she goes out to gather food she works less energetically than formerly, often stopping to rest on the leaf of a tree or on a blade of grass. As soon as she finds that her children are able to collect sufficient honey and pollen for the maintenance of the little family, she relinquishes this labour, and henceforth devotes herself entirely to indoor duties ...
Frederick Sladen, 1912, The Humble-bee

Later in the year the queen begins to lay unfertilised eggs which develop into males. It is this peculiar system of sex-determination that allows many bees, wasps and ants to adopt their social way of life. In contrast to most animals, it makes better evolutionary sense for a female bee to look after her sisters than to breed herself - in short, a female bee is more closely related to her sisters than to her offspring. At the same time, some of the last fertilised eggs develop into new queens.

The males spend a short life lounging around on flower-heads (thistles are especially favoured because the bees do not need to move too far between sips), drinking lots of nectar and mating with any young queens they can attract. This dissolute behaviour is, to be fair, more obvious than their complex social behaviour involving scent-marking vegetation and patrolling along well-defined routes. Eventually, all bees in the colony except the young mated queens die, and these, after having built up their fat reserves, dig into the ground to hibernate until spring.

This daily marking of the route accounts for the fact that males will desert some of the points visited on the previous day and include new ones.

When laying down scent the males grip the leaves, twigs or pieces of bark they are scent-marking in their mandibles and make gnawing movements, often simultaneously whirring their wings in an excited manner. There can be little doubt that the biological function of these flight-routes of male bumblebees is to ensure that any nubile queen of the same species ... quickly finds a mate.
Free & Butler, 1959, Bumblebees

Colony size and the length of the life-cycle differ between species, and are dependent on environment (altitude, latitude and habitat). In some northern areas, nests may produce few workers - possibly none at all - because of the shortness of the season and shortage of food. In more southern areas, colonies may produce several hundred workers, and some species may have more than one generation in a year.

The factors determining whether fertilised eggs are laid, and whether workers or queens develop from them, vary with species, but food supply, chemical communication and queen behaviour all contribute.

Cuckoo Bumblebees

As always in nature, if there is the chance to exploit the other animals and plants around, something will do just that. Just as avian cuckoos exploit the parental instincts of 'normal' birds, cuckoo bumblebees take advantage of the social structure of the 'normal' bumblebees. Cuckoo bumblebee females emerge from hibernation rather later than their hosts, and begin to search for the scent of a newly-established nest of their favoured bumblebee host. On finding one - which at that stage will contain only the host queen, perhaps a few workers, and developing host larvae - the cuckoo queen enters the nest. Cuckoo bees have a thicker and tougher cuticle than the host bees, and this may prevent them from being stung to death by the host queen. The cuckoo female then lays her own eggs to be cared for by the host workers. Cuckoo bumblebees have no workers of their own, so their eggs develop either into breeding females or males. As with normal bumblebees, the males die in autumn, and only the fertilised females survive the winter in hibernation.

Female Gypsy Cuckoo Bumblebee (*Psithyrus bohemicus*) on a thistle head

The Gypsy Cuckoo Bumblebee (*Bombus bohemicus*) breeds in nests of the White-tailed Bumblebee

Cuckoo bumblebees have no pollen baskets, and never forage for the colony. All the food they collect is for their own use. Each species of cuckoo bumblebee has its own special host bumblebee. There is sometimes a resemblance in colour between cuckoo and host, though its significance to the insects is not clear. The same behaviour appears in other social insects - there are cuckoo wasps and cuckoo ants, for example.

Although the queen bees try to sting this foreign intruder, her very thick coat of mail prevents them,

and in a short while, when enough worker bees are hatched to keep the colony alive, the Usurper Bee stings the queen to death, usurps her place and commences laying eggs which are destined to become Apathus drones and females. The poor Humble Bees, working blindly against their own interests, rear up the young Apathus grubs, which undergo precisely the same changes of growth as they.

Frederick Sladen, 1892, writing of cuckoo bumblebees, which he called 'usurper bees' with the Latin name Apathus.

13

How they fly
and why they sting

How they fly

There is a long-standing belief that scientific laws prove that bumblebees should not be able to fly. This resembles another famous story that dolphins and whales should not be able to swim as fast as they clearly do. Both stories are based on the same kind of misunderstanding.

A Garden Bumblebee (*Bombus hortorum*) flies to a foxglove flower, long tongue extended

If you measure the mass and wing area of a bumblebee and make calculations familiar to any aeronautical engineer, you conclude that bumblebees cannot glide. However, insects are not gliders - their wings change shape and angle as they flap. This can be clearly seen on the Contents page, where the wings have turned upside-down, with the rear edge of the wing leading!

The flight of insects is extremely complicated to describe in detail, and it is only relatively recently that the story has been worked out, with the help of tethered insects in wind tunnels and a few drifts of smoke to show the movements of the air. By flapping their wings, insects generate eddies of air which support their weight. The interaction of the air with the wings is completely consistent with the laws of physics, so science says that bumblebees can fly - as long as they flap their wings! Indeed they fly very effectively, as they can carry a load of pollen and nectar equal to more than half of their unladen body weight.

14

The bumblebee as a flying machine

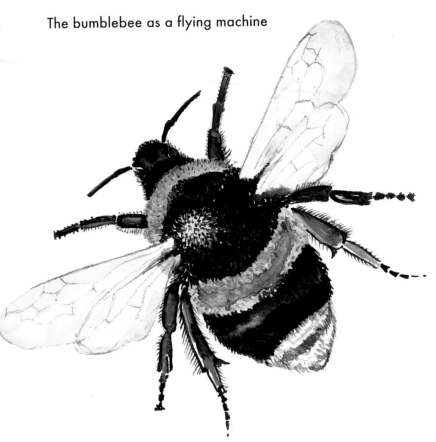

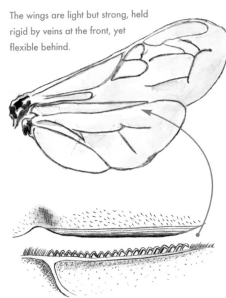

The wings are light but strong, held rigid by veins at the front, yet flexible behind.

The front wing has a fold, which engages with a beautifully precise row of hooks to link the two into a single surface.

Hairs designed to hold pollen also retain heat, to let muscles work efficiently.

Powerful muscles act on a complex 'spring loaded' skeleton to flap the wings up to 200 times every second. This creates eddies that support the bee's weight and also thrust forces that can move it forward at more than 20km/per hour.

Why they sting

One of the best known characteristics of bumblebees, and the least helpful in terms of their public relations, is their ability to sting. The sting is a modified part of the female reproductive system - the ovipositor, or tube used for laying the eggs - which has taken over this new rôle. An obvious consequence is that males do not sting. All females - workers and queens - can sting, but stings are not primarily offensive weapons.

Bumblebees are not aggressive insects. Left alone, they mind their own business and get on with the important things in life. Even if disturbed at the nest, bumblebees will not usually attack like honeybees or social wasps. They can, however, retaliate if they perceive that they are under attack.

If a bumblebee is physically threatened, even unintentionally as one puts a hand on an unseen bee in the grass, it may sting. And who could blame it for that? For most people, the effect of the sting is mild, though for anyone with an allergic hypersensitivity the dangers will be real. The main effect comes, not from the penetration, but from the variety of chemicals forming the venom which is forcibly injected under the skin. These damage cell structure, causing pain and inflammation.

Bumblebees have only tiny barbs on the sting, so unlike honeybees they can withdraw the sting without injury to themselves.

Normally, a bumblebee will sting only if severely provoked by a predator or invader at the nest. A badger will think twice if its snout is treated to a sting or two, and may look for a less painful way to feed. The one occasion where a sting is routinely used offensively is when a female cuckoo bumblebee attempts to take over a host nest. The queens may fight and try to sting each other to death. The female cuckoo bumblebee has evolved an especially tough armour which gives her an advantage in that situation.

Humble Bees, like Wasps, can sting as many times as they like, without dying, but their stings are slight, and the effects sooner over than those of either bees or wasps. Only Terrestris & Lapidarius will, when disturbed, take to the wing and quietly make straight for their enemy. Muscorum & Sylvarum lie on their backs ready to clutch & sting any foreign body that approaches near enough. The remaining species, when their nest is taken, will simply fly away to return when the plunderer has departed.
Frederick Sladen, 1892

16

Where they live

Bumblebee habitat

Unlike most insects, but in common with the ants and social wasps, bumblebees have a fixed base - the nest - around which all activities must be undertaken, in some populations for as long as seven months. The White-tailed Bumblebee, for example, may emerge in March, and still have active colonies in October. This means that all their needs must exist during all that time within easy flying distance of the nest.

Apart from the nest-site itself, the most important component of the habitat is forage. It is not enough that there are abundant flowers. Each species of bumblebee has its own favoured menu, so the flowers must be appropriate. There must be a continuous supply of flowers - no 'hungry gap' - throughout the season. The flowers should be present within 1-2km of the nest to reduce the time and energy expended, although some bees will travel much longer distances. Finally, the flowers must be present in sufficient density to allow efficient collection of pollen or nectar.

Bumblebees prefer to forage at perennial plants - few annuals provide appropriate food - so the best habitats are mixed, long-established, and relatively undisturbed. Many such places occur on the edges of larger tracts of woods or fields, along roadsides and in gardens.

None of our bumblebees is dependent on a single species of plant for pollen. Different species, however, show strong (but not exclusive) associations with particular plants.

Hedgerows hold many excellent forage plants

This beautiful roadside verge in Orkney provides food for a variety of bumblebees

Hedges and edges

Shrubs and trees in an old hedge may not be used much as forage, but the plants associated with them may be very important. Bramble and wild raspberry, foxglove, vetches, thistles, honeysuckle - all are excellent food sources. These same plants often grow in abundance in the rides and at the edges of forests, where, because forestry is a long-term industry, they can flourish undisturbed for years. Forest roads are among the best places to find males of the Forest Cuckoo Bumblebee in late summer feeding lazily on abundant spear and marsh thistles.

The disturbed ground along the verges of our major roads is often a rich source of food. White clover, red clover and bird's-foot trefoil grow in abundance. These plants are excellent sources of pollen and nectar, and can support large numbers of White-tailed and Garden Bumblebees as well as being stunningly beautiful.

Old diverse hedgerows and field edges were common before intensification of farming. In some parts of Scotland, removal of hedges and ploughing of fields right up to the boundaries has removed large areas of wild flowers, and with them the insect populations which relied on them. Agri-environment schemes can be used to redress this problem by encouraging areas on farms to be left unploughed and so encourage wild plants and insects, but there is still a long way to go. Most of our common species can be found in such places - frequently six or more species foraging together.

Heath, moor and mountain

Although many species of bumblebee will forage on heath or moorland, the habitat is especially associated with the beautiful Bilberry Bumblebee and its less distinctive cousin, the Heath Bumblebee.

Queens of the Bilberry Bumblebee have long been thought to depend on the flowers of the bilberry or blaeberry (as it is known in Scotland). This dependence has recently been demonstrated, with the queens feeding at blaeberry when little else is available. This bee is causing concern throughout Britain, as it seems to have declined on, or even been lost from, many of its former sites. The quality of blaeberry on a moor is affected by land management. Grazing by sheep and deer can reduce the abundance of the flowers, while blaeberry may become temporarily dominant after moorland is burned.

Moorland is especially useful to the Bilberry Bumblebee if there is a good supply of bird's-foot trefoil (or 'bacon-and-eggs' as it is also known), perhaps on river shingles, eroding banks, or nearby basic grassland, to provide forage for the workers.

Bilberry Bumblebee Bombus monticola

In June, when the flowering bell heather and cross-leaved heath turn the landscape from brown to purple and pink, the Heath Bumblebee gets busy. Queens establish nests with their pollen, and rear workers in time for the real bonanza in August and September - ling heather. This bee is probably able to exist on just these three species, although in practice early queens find sustenance from lousewort and other less abundant plants. Higher in the mountains or near the coast, if the heaths are scarce, queens use wild thyme in the early season instead.

Later in the season, all the moorland bees, especially males, use another common moorland plant - the devil's-bit scabious.

Both the Bilberry Bumblebee and Heath Bumblebee are found right to the tops of our highest mountains, keeping company with mountain hare, ptarmigan and dotterel.

Heathery moors are the main habitat of the Heath Bumblebee (*Bombus jonellus*)

Machair

The machair grassland based on the calcareous shell-sand of the west coast of the Western Isles is famed for its wealth of flowers. In summer, a riot of colour - red and white of the clover, yellow of the kidney-vetch, purple of the tufted vetch and knapweed - indicates a vastly important habitat for flower-loving insects. It stands in stark contrast to the relatively flower-poor acid moorland inland.

It is no surprise that machair holds some very special bumblebees. The Great Yellow Bumblebee is common in its main remaining British stronghold, and a race of the Moss Carder Bee which is confined to the Atlantic fringe of the British Isles is widespread throughout the Western Isles. These bees thrive among the flower-rich acres in which the corncrake also survives. Like the corncrake, the Great Yellow Bumblebee was once widespread over the mainland of Scotland and England, but the advance of intensive farming has pushed it to the northern and western edges of the country in the Hebrides, Orkney, Caithness and Sutherland (see maps on page 27).

Machair is usually close to ranker vegetation in sand dunes or untrimmed banks and verges where bees can find nest-sites in rodent burrows or grass tussocks.

Black knapweed is important for the rare Great Yellow Bumblebee (*Bombus distinguendus*)

22

The flowers on the machair of the Western Isles support an abundance of rare bumblebees

Gardens

Much wildlife conservation concentrates on re-establishing natural habitats that have been degraded or lost, but artificial habitats are important too, and, where bumblebees are concerned, the most important of these must be gardens.

For an insect dependent on flowers, a diverse garden must be the nearest thing to perfect bliss. Over 60 species of hoverfly and 13 species of bumblebee have been found in one village garden in the Highlands. A single garden in Aberdeen has been visited by 10 species of bumblebee. In most parts of Scotland, a well-stocked garden will attract six or more species.

A garden offering suitable flowers between March and October extends the foraging season. Gardens provide forage before suitable wild flowers have appeared, and after the wild crop has finished. In northern areas, where summer is notoriously short, this is especially important. With a lot of food in a small area, the bees do not waste energy flying long distances between flowers.

But not any garden will do. If pesticides are used, there is a chance that bumblebees will be adversely affected. Most importantly, the flowers must attract the insects and allow them to reach the pollen and nectar inside.

One major problem comes from modification of flowers to make them more attractive to the human eye. Hybrids may not produce pollen. Mutant double blooms have petals or other flower parts multiplied unnaturally or misshapen. It is no surprise that the finely-evolved relationship matching insect to flower is destroyed by such changes, and many modified flowers do not let the bees reach the nectar. For insects, the simplest and most natural flowers are best. (For examples see page 28.)

There is no better place for collecting humble-bees than a large old-fashioned garden. Of the scores of cultivated flowers that they delight in ... globe artichoke (I have seen as many as fourteen humble-bees on one flower-head of this plant), also raspberry and fruit blossom of all kinds ...
Frederick Sladen, 1912, The Humble-bee

A garden like this will attract bumblebees and many other insects

Threats

The biggest threat to bumblebees in Britain is habitat loss and fragmentation. There is no danger from predators or disease, and humans do not persecute them deliberately. Therefore, it is important to maintain suitable habitats throughout Scotland so that bumblebees can continue to thrive.

Over the past 50 years, several British species of bumblebee have declined markedly. One English species has become extinct. In Scotland we have been luckier, but we cannot be complacent, especially as we now hold a significant proportion of the UK populations of some species.

Four species of bumblebee in Scotland - the Bilberry Bumblebee, Moss Carder Bee, Red-shanked Carder Bee and Great Yellow Bumblebee - give cause for concern. A common feature of their decline is the loss of extensive flower-rich habitats that comes with increasing intensification of land use for agriculture, forestry and development.

Another pressure which may prove to be a problem is climate change. As weather patterns change, there are effects on the insects themselves and on their favoured habitats and forage plants. At present, the potential effects of climate change are much debated, but we may see decreases among some of our more northern and upland species at the same time as gaining others from the south.

In 2001 a continental bumblebee (Bombus hypnorum) arrived in England for the first time and is now breeding. Two species, the Buff-tailed and Red-tailed Bumblebees, have recently spread into the Highlands from southern Scotland, though it is not clear that this is related to trends in climate. The Red-tailed Bumblebee has shown great changes in distribution in Scotland before, and we do not understand what precise climatic factors determine the distribution of these insects.

The Great Yellow Bumblebee (*Bombus distinguendus*) has been lost from much of Britain in the last hundred years

Distribution before 1975 from *Atlas of the Bumblebees of the British Isles, ITE, 1980.* Maps prepared with DMAP.

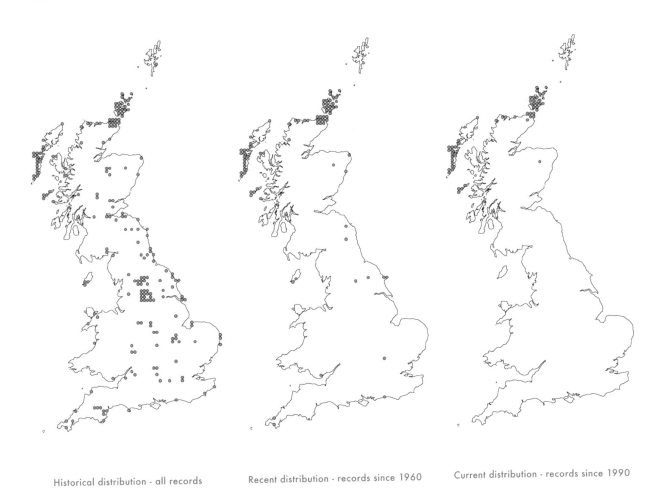

Historical distribution - all records   Recent distribution - records since 1960   Current distribution - records since 1990

27

Conservation - how you can help bumblebees

Gardeners

Gardens should provide plenty of spring and autumn forage. The list suggests some plants that will improve the value of any garden for bumblebees, but gardeners will soon discover what plants in their own plots are equally attractive. A 'wild patch' - conservation in the garden can be a wonderful excuse for laziness - allows brambles, wild raspberries, foxgloves and vetches to thrive, while rank grass can provide nest sites.

A bumblebee nest-box

Simple nest-boxes for bumblebees can be made from plant-pots buried in a patch of ground which will remain undisturbed, with a tube from the pot to the surface allowing the bees to come in and out. Ready-made boxes are available commercially.

Some bumblebee plants for gardens

Spring and early summer	Summer	Late summer and autumn
winter heath	raspberry	borage
flowering currant	bramble	ice-plant
willow	wild rose	woundwort
lungwort	thyme	monk's-hood
pieris	sage	snowberry
gean (wild cherry)	marjoram	bistort
rhododendron	lavender	tutsan
sycamore	catmint	
maple	purple loosestrife	
yellow archangel	clovers	
bugle	vetches	
perennial cornflower	broad bean	
bistort	foxglove	
broom	stonecrop	
	honeysuckle	
	buddleia	
	thistles	
	scabious	
	chives	
	columbine	

Flowering currant

Buddleia

Honeysuckle

Borage

Farmers and crofters

Farmers can take advantage of agricultural grants to enhance their land for wildlife. For bumblebees, short term set-aside of large areas may not be as good as leaving narrower strips and hedges for longer, which allows perennials to establish. Any farming practice that encourages perennial flowers, whether rotation on a 3 or 4 year cycle, or preservation of field edges, or cropping hay in the traditional way, will encourage bumblebees and other wildlife.

The biggest conflict between livestock farming and bumblebees comes through grazing. Sheep are such efficient grazers that even fields with a diverse flora are rendered useless to bumblebees because the plants are prevented from flowering. Cattle-rearing as traditionally practised in the Western Isles can be much less damaging, and is a valuable tool in the conservation of the Great Yellow Bumblebee.

In August, when their numbers are greatest and wild flowers begin to fade, they flock to the fields of red clover, and the lazy males congregate on the thistle heads.
Frederick Sladen, 1912, The Humble-bee

Traditional farming methods can produce meadows like this one in Perthshire

Foresters

All woodland managers should take into account the importance of the edges of plantations and the banks of forest roads. These often hold good populations of thistles and foxglove which are used extensively by cuckoo bumblebees and the Garden Bumblebee respectively. Thickets of bramble and wild raspberry are used by almost any bumblebee that finds them, and are especially important to the Early Bumblebee.

The Forest Cuckoo Bumblebee (*Bombus sylvestris*) is usually found on forest roads or edges

31

Foxgloves in a forest ride will attract Garden Bumblebees

Local Authorities

It has been claimed that roadside verges form one of our biggest nature reserves. Yet so often these are mowed to remove flowering vegetation when it is at its most beautiful to humans and its most useful to insects. There is the chance through Local Biodiversity Action Plans to implement a more wildlife-friendly approach to verge cutting, perhaps by identifying stretches of particular richness, or by altering the time of trimming to allow the important plants to flower and set seed freely. Interested individuals can alert councillors and officials to verges that deserve protection where safety is not compromised.

The same principles apply to 'waste ground', an unhelpful name to the cause of conservation. A better name would be 'temporary wildlife refuge'. Where areas of disturbed ground are left for several years, a diverse flora develops and attracts a corresponding variety of insects.

In planning public places, councils could specify appropriate bee-friendly landscaping and ornamental planting, using native plants from the locality. This would be especially useful in urban areas where wild forage may be scarce.

The needs of bumblebees should be considered when planting in public spaces

Finding out more about bumblebees

Societies

The Bees, Wasps and Ants Recording Society (BWARS).
www.bwars.com

Biological Recording in Scotland (BRISC).
www.brisc.org.uk

International Bee Research Association (IBRA),
18 North Road, Cardiff CF10 3DT. www.ibra.org.uk

There are also many Local Biological Records Centres
(details from the BRISC website), as well as local clubs
and societies with a general interest in natural history.

Classic works

Free, J. and Butler, C. 1959. *Bumblebees*. Collins. (Out of
print but available in libraries.)

Sladen, F.W.L. 1989. *The Humble-bee, its Life History and
how to Domesticate it*, Logaston Press. (A recent edition
of the original 1912 book, also containing a reproduction
of his 1892 hand-written booklet.)

Identification Guides

Benton, T. 2000. *The Bumblebees of Essex*. Lopinga
Books. (This book contains much detail on bumblebee
biology as well as technical identification keys.)

Chinery, M. 1986. *Collins Guide to the Insects of Britain
and Western Europe*. Collins.

Prŷs-Jones, O. and Corbet, S. 1991. *Bumblebees*,
Richmond. (This book contains much detail on bumblebee
biology as well as technical identification keys).

Bumblebee biology (also see above)

Goulson, D. 2003. *Bumblebees - their behaviour and
ecology*. Oxford University Press.

O'Toole, C. 2002. *Bumblebees*. Osmia Publications.

Pollination

Proctor, M. Yeo, P. and Lack, A. 1996. *The natural history
of pollination*. HarperCollins.

Also in the Naturally Scottish series...

If you have enjoyed Red Kites why not find out more about Scotland's wildlife in our Naturally Scottish series. Each booklet looks at one or more of Scotland's native species. The clear and informative text is illustrated with exceptional photographs by top wildlife photographers, showing the species in their native habitats and illustrating their relationships with man. They also provide information on conservation and the law.

Burnet Moths

Unlike many other species of moth, burnet moths fly by day. They can be easily recognised by their beautiful, glossy black wings with crimson spots. Their striking colouring is a very real warning to predators.
Mark Young
ISBN 1 85397 209 6 pbk 24pp £3.00

Corncrakes

Secretive, skulking, rasping, loud, tuneless, scarce. . . all these words have been used to describe the corncrake. But once you could have added plentiful and widespread to the list. Now only a few birds visit Scotland each year. This booklet brings you the latest information on the corncrake and reveals this elusive and noisy bird in its grassy home.
Rhys Green & Helen Riley
ISBN 1 85397 049 2 pbk 40pp £3.95

Fungi

Fungi belong to one of the most varied, useful and ancient kingdoms in the natural world. Scotland may have almost 2000 larger species with some of the most interesting found in our woodlands and grasslands. This booklet provides an introduction to their life cycles, habitats and conservation. Discover the fascinating forms of earthstars, truffles and waxcaps.
Roy Watling MBE and Stephen Ward
ISBN 1 85397 341 6 pbk 40pp £4.95

Red Kite

This graceful and distinctive bird was absent from Scotland's skies for more than a century. Now, with the help of a successful programme of re-introduction, it's russet plumage and forked tail can once again be seen in Scotland.
David Minns and Doug Gilbert
ISBN 1 85397 210 X pbk 24pp £3.00

Red Squirrels

The red squirrel is one Scotland's most endearing mammals. This booklet provides an insight into their ecology and some of the problems facing red squirrels in Scotland today.
Peter Lurz & Mairi Cooper
ISBN 1 85397 298 4 pbk 20pp £3.00

River Runners

Scotland's clean, cascading rivers contain a fascinating array of species. The atlantic salmon is the best known of our riverine species but others, such as lampreys and freshwater pearl mussels, are frequently overlooked but no less captivating. This booklet aims to illuminate aspects of their intriguing and largely unseen lifecycles, habitats and conservation measures.
Iain Sime
ISBN 1 85397 353 X

Sea Eagles

This magnificent bird, with its wing span of over 2m is the largest bird of prey in Britain. In 1916 they became extinct, but a reintroduction programme began in 1975. This booklet documents the return of this truly majestic eagle. Production subsidised by Anheuser-Busch.
Greg Mudge, Kevin Duffy, Kate Thompson & John Love
ISBN 1 85397 208 8 pbk 16pp £1.50

SNH Publications Order Form:
Naturally Scottish Series

Title	Price	Quantity
Burnet Moths	£3.00	....
Corncrakes	£3.95	....
Fungi	£4.95	....
Red Kites	£3.95	....
Red Squirrels	£3.00	....
River Runners	£4.95	....
Sea Eagles	£1.50	....

Postage and packing: free of charge in the UK, a standard charge of £2.95 will be applied to all orders from the European Union. Elsewhere a standard charge of £5.50 will be applied for postage.

Please complete in BLOCK CAPITALS

Name _____

Address _____

_____

_____

Post Code

Type of Credit Card   VISA ☐   MasterCard ☐

Name of card holder _____

Card Number ☐☐☐☐ ☐☐☐☐ ☐☐☐☐ ☐☐☐☐

Expiry Date ☐☐ ☐☐

Send order and cheque made payable to Scottish Natural Heritage to:

Scottish Natural Heritage. Design and Publications, Battleby, Redgorton, Perth PH1 3EW

pubs@redgore.demon.co.uk

www.snh.org.uk

Please add my name to the mailing list for the: SNH Magazine ☐

Publications Catalogue ☐